Stretching For Success Workbook

7 Steps to STRETCH Beyond Your Comfort Zone and Harness Your Power in Life and Work

SONAL SHETH ZAWAHRI

Stretching For Success Workbook:
7 Steps to STRETCH Beyond Your Comfort Zone and Harness Your Power in Life and Work
Copyright © 2020 Sonal Sheth Zawahri

ISBN:978-1-7351349-1-8

Enhanced
DNA
DEVELOP. NURTURE. ACHIEVE.
Publishing Division

DenolaBurton@EnhancedDNA1.com
www.EnhancedDNAPublishing.com

Tru You Crew Acknowledgements

At Tru You, I take great pride in, and give gratitude for, those who have been and continue to be an integral part of my journey. Thank you to the following humans for helping me make this workbook possible:

Cover Design and Illustrated by: Nnenna Jemie and Bethany Berghofer
Edited by: Amber Peckham
Thinking Partner: Aisha Cargile
Graphics: Nathaniel Grady

The best way to thank others is to be an ambassador for them. Please spread the word and call on these folks so that you can experience their greatness yourself. To find their contact information, visit:

https://www.sonalshethzawahri.com/the-crew

To Mommy and Daddy
For having the courage and fortitude to stretch out of their comfort zone
and come to America 49 years ago, to raise us in Brooklyn, and to bring us to
the Midwest. You never gave up. Your resilience and positive outlook on life
is what inspires me to never give up.
You are my inspiration.

To my husband and daughter, thank you for your support, love, and
patience while mommy pursues her passion.

Table of Contents

WHAT DOES IT MEAN TO

stretch?

/'streCH/-verb

1 : To step out of one's comfort zone.

see also: "where the magic happens"

"harness the power"

Introduction

A great place to start...

We often hear people (and sometimes our own inner voice) tell us to stretch out of our comfort zone. I tell my clients all the time, "It is in this space of discomfort that we can experience growth and change, as long as we are listening." But what does this even mean? How do we relate this to our personal and professional lives today? How can we measure our success if we choose to stretch? Who can hold us accountable?

These are great questions that we will reveal in this workbook. This workbook will allow you to learn how to step into the best version of you by utilizing simple activities that can be done individually or in a team environment and in a short amount of time (without spending a lot of time on it).

The order of the chapters below is intentional. We start with an understanding of self and creating a foundation, before shifting to improving our ability to understand and better interact with others.

We will first start by identifying our *comfort zone* and then learn how each of us can set goals and intentions to stretch in a way that will yield results. Not necessarily immediate results, but results that will contribute to our growth.

What to look for in this workbook:

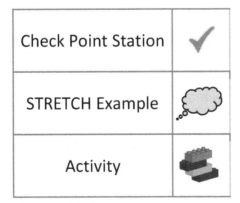
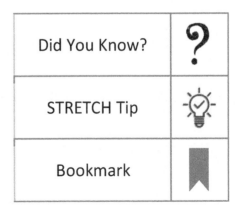

In the space below, please brainstorm what words come to mind when you think about *Comfort Zone.*

"If you want something you've never had, then you've got to do something you've never done!" – Unknown

1. Define what you think is meant by a comfort zone? What does the previous quote mean in the context of your answers?

_____

_____

_____

2. Identify a situation where you have remained in your comfort zone when you were given an opportunity to try something new? What made you stay in your comfort zone?

	Situation	What made you stay?
Personally		
Professionally		
Socially		
Physically		
Spiritually		
Other		

3. What was the outcome of staying in that comfort zone?

_____

_____

_____

In this workbook you will have the opportunity to identify something personally or professionally that will require you to possibly step out of your comfort zone and step into your *STRETCH*.

This workbook is a tool that will introduce you to a process that will allow you to implement the **S.T.R.E.T.C.H.** model in your personal and professional roles. The next 7 sections will take you through each of the steps to stretching and help you create a plan and execute it to achieve your goal(s).

Let's get started...

S is for Self-Awareness

According to the dictionary, *Self-Awareness /ˈˌself əˈwernəs/ noun*
  1. *conscious knowledge of one's own character, feelings, motives, and desires.*

The value of being self-aware

What is the value of knowing who you are and how you are perceived by others?

Self-awareness allows us to better understand ourselves and what motivates us. With this knowledge, we are then empowered to make changes to build up our areas of strength and acknowledge those areas where improvement is needed.

Self-awareness is about learning to better understand why you feel what you feel and why you behave in a particular way. Once you begin to understand this concept you then have the opportunity and freedom to change things about yourself, enabling you to create a life that you want. ***It's almost impossible to change and become self-accepting if you are unsure as to who you are.*** Having clarity about who you are and what you want can be empowering, giving you the confidence to make changes.

When we are not transparent about what we don't know and where we need help, we can set ourselves up for relationships that lack trust and integrity. If we are not being honest with ourselves, it does eventually show through to others and they will find it difficult to trust our opinion and knowledge in future circumstances.

When someone has a high level of self-awareness, it allows them to show up confident in their abilities and self-worth, enabling them to step into action and successfully achieve goals. This is because they know where they excel, where they need improvement, and where they are better off relying on the skills and expertise of others.

Self-awareness is the first step in setting goals. When we are conscious of what we are good at and what areas we still need improvement in, we are better able to tackle what we need to get done.

It is my intention to help you to become more self-aware. And then use that self-awareness to identify what it is you want to change and determine what your stretch will be.

So, how do we develop self-awareness? According to positivepsychology.com, *"developing self-awareness requires higher-level cognitive processing. It requires an information-gathering perspective. This processing results in increases in adaptability and flexibility. Having increased self-awareness builds resilience."*

In order to understand who we are and how we work, we get to ask ourselves some important questions, like...Who am I? What am I feeling? What am I doing? How am I showing up? What do I want to change? What is my goal?

So, let's gather some information about ourselves. Let's start by identifying who you are NOW.

 Sonal's Stretch Example:

Self-Awareness: *I want to learn how to manage my time better as a mom, wife, daughter, and entrepreneur.* **Future state**: *When I have learned to manage my time better, this is what it looks like for me: I will be able to be fully present in whichever role I am in. I am energized and ready to deliver in any of these roles; entrepreneur, mom, wife, and daughter. How will I measure my outcome in the end?*

1. *When I have prioritized my tasks for the day in a way that is best for my life that day*
2. *When I consistently feel present and focused on the task at hand*
3. *When I am consistently achieving the priority items on my calendar 5 days out of 7.*
4. *When I am accomplishing goals in one of my roles without feeling frazzled across all 4 roles.*

Emotional Intelligence and Self-Awareness

Accurate	Diplomatic	Industrious	Punctual
Active	Distracted	Impartial	Rational
Adaptable	Dishonest	Innovative	Relational
Adept	Dynamic	Intuitive	Reliable
Adaptable	Dependable	Inventive	Reserved
Adventurous	Determined	Jealous	Resourceful
Affectionate	Diplomatic	Joyful	Scientific
Ambitious	Discreet	Knowledgeable	Self-Confident
Amiable	Emotional	Lazy	Self-Disciplined
Aggressive	Empathetic	Lively	Sensible
Analytical	Egotistical	Logical	Sociable
Anxious	Energetic	Loyal	Sincere
Arrogant	Enthusiastic	Mature	Selfish
Artistic	Extroverted	Methodical	Smart
Articulate	Exuberant	Motivated	Serious
Bossy	Efficient	Meticulous	Supportive
Brave	Enterprising	Mean	Sympathetic
Broad-minded	Experienced	Nervous	Stubborn
Calculating	Fearless	Optimistic	Sense of humor
Competent	Flexible	Objective	Sensitive
Conscientious	Friendly	Outgoing	Sincere
Constructive	Funny	Orderly	Successful
Creative	Fair	Personable	Systematic
Calm	Firm	Pleasant	Unassuming
Charismatic	Happy	Positive	Tactful
Creative	Honest	Proficient	Talkative
Compassionate	Humble	Productive	Timid
Conscientious	Genuine	Passionate	Thoughtful
Considerate	Generous	Patience	Trustworthy
Courageous	Gregarious	Pessimistic	Worried
Courteous	Imaginative	Persistent	Warm-Hearted
Cheerful	Inpatient	Philosophical	Upbeat
Dependable	Impulsive	Popular	Versatile
Determined	Intellectual	Practical	Witty
Devious	Intelligent	Proud	
Diligent	Introverted	Productive	

Self-Awareness Activity

Identifying who you are now

Step 1: Describing Yourself

Please take a look at the list of adjectives provided on the previous page. Please choose *3 adjectives* from the list that best describes how you show up in your life on a day to day basis (not how you want to show up).

Three (3) Adjectives that best describes me today:

1. _____

2. _____

3. _____

Tip:
If working with one or more individuals, share your 3 adjectives and explain why you chose those adjectives

Step 2: Most Dominant Trait

Now, if you were to choose which of these three adjectives best describes you as you are today, which one would it be?

Most Dominant Trait:

_____

Tip:
If you are working with one or more individuals, share your most dominant trait with them. If working with a group of leaders and individuals, add your dominant trait to your name badge or outside of your cubicle for everyone to see.

Step 3: Are you where you want to be?

NOW...from the previous list of adjectives please choose 3 words that best describe how you **want** to show up in your life on a day to day basis.

What three (3) adjectives best describe how you **WANT** to show up:

1. _____

2. _____

3. _____

Please take a moment to self-reflect:

Were the list of adjectives the same or different in Step 1 vs. Step 3?

YES	NO

What were the differences? Why do you think that is?

_____

_____

_____

_____

_____

_____

What you have done here, is to identify where you are currently and where you want to be. This is being self-aware and identifying goals.

Now that you've executed this process once, let's do it again to determine what our **S.T.R.E.T.C.H.©** goal is going to be by answering the following questions:

1. Based on your previous answers, where are you in your current mindset?

   _____

   _____

   _____

2. How do you visualize your ideal future mindset? (Describe it. What does it look like in your mind)?

   _____

   _____

   _____

3. In what areas do you need to make improvements to get you from your current mindset to your future mindset?

   _____

   _____

   _____

4. What new skills or traits do you want to acquire in order to get to your future?

   _____

   _____

   _____

Your response to question #4 will be your **S.T.R.E.T.C.H.©** goal for this workbook. These 7 steps will be a tool you can consistently use to successfully identify and achieve your objectives that lie outside of your comfort zone.

 Check Point Station: *At the end of each section, we will summarize where we are in our STRETCH process.*

S: Self-Awareness (Identifying what matters to you)

You now have a better understanding of who you are and where you are focusing your energy and improvement efforts. Let's move on to the next step and develop a plan to stay on track.

T is for *Tone* (Set the Tone)

In the previous section, we covered **S** for *Self-Awareness* where you had the opportunity to do some self-reflection and thoughtful brainstorming in order to allow you to have a clearer mental image of *who you are now* versus *who you want to be.* We then ended the previous section by identifying your **S.T.R.E.T.C.H.** goal. Please take a moment to re-state your **S.T.R.E.T.C.H.** goal below.

Stretch Example:
I want to learn how to manage my time better as a mom, wife, daughter, and entrepreneur.

Your S.T.R.E.T.C.H. goal:

_____

_____

_____

_____

Where are you now?
The intention is now to have a better understanding of who you are and where you are focusing your energy and improvement efforts. Let's move on to the next step and develop a plan to stay on track.

The value behind setting a tone or an attitude towards a goal that we set, can be a game-changer. Have you ever set a goal or an intention but you find yourself dragging your feet to get it done? You begrudgingly continue on with the plan even when you don't see immediate results? And then, you get to the goal but you're not satisfied with the outcome because your heart wasn't into it. How can you regain the initial passion for your goal so that you can complete it without burnout?

When I used to think of tone, I would think of attitude. How can you shift your attitude and approach towards this goal?

Before we answer some of these questions, let's identify the difference between tone and attitude.

Tone and attitude are so closely related. Attitude can generally refer to the characteristics that a person has and tone refers to how they are delivering their message. The tone of a text can suggest the writer's attitude toward her subject and/or audience.

Tone gives shape and life to a conversation, both through written and verbal discussion. It is through tone, that the attitude and mood of a conversation are created and presented. It gives voice to the characters, both literally and figuratively.

What's powerful is that the behaviors we adopt in any given situation are the direct result of our attitude, mindset, knowledge, and skills that we choose to have.

In this section, we will give you an opportunity to look at the attitude you have towards your *S.T.R.E.T.C.H.* goal and provide tools to help you think more positively and constructively, thereby, setting the tone for your efforts. While attitude is how you feel, the tone is how you come across, even to yourself. By deliberately setting your tone when you start working on your *S.T.R.E.T.C.H.* goal you can consistently encourage yourself to show up in a way to maximize your chances of success. Choose an attitude and tone that will empower you in times of discouragement and will allow you to stay in action.

Stretch Example:

Self-Awareness: *I want to learn how to manage my time better as a mom, wife, daughter, and entrepreneur.* **Future state***: When I have learned to manage my time better, this is what it looks like for me: I will be able to be fully present in whichever role I am in. I am energized and ready to deliver in any of these roles; entrepreneur, mom, wife, and daughter. How will I measure my outcome in the end?*

1. *When I have prioritized my tasks for the day in a way that is best for my life that day*
2. *When I consistently feel present and focused on the task at hand*
3. *When I am consistently achieving the priority items on my calendar 5 days out of 7.*
4. *When I am accomplishing goals in one of my roles without feeling frazzled across all 4 roles.*

Tone: *I can choose my attitude and set my tone. Every day I can start my day by looking at my calendar or creating my to-do list. And ensure that I praise and/or reward myself for completing this step towards better managing my time. For those days where I do not achieve this step, I can set the intention to remind myself that tomorrow is a new day and I* **get to** *do better.*

	<u>Tone Activity</u>
	Determine the attitude and tone that works for you

This is where the real work begins and consistency comes in. But you get to decide what that looks like. Here you can only be guided so much because the answers to the following questions are ones only you and those closest to you know.

1. How do you visualize your ideal future mindset? (Describe it. What does it look like in your mind)?

   _____

   _____

   _____

1. What type of reinforcement works best for you? Choose all that apply:
   - ☐ External (Reinforcement provided by an external source)
   - ☐ Internal (Reinforcement you provide yourself)
   - ☐ Verbal praise (Ex: I did well today. You did well today. Way to go!)
   - ☐ Tangible reward (Something you can see, touch, spend, etc.)
   - ☐ Results based encouragement (You achieved a milestone, Nice job!)
   - ☐ Competition based (You beat yesterday's time. You broke the record. Etc.)
   - ☐ Other: _____

2. How frequently do you need reinforcement to keep motivated? (Ex: daily, weekly, monthly, etc.)?

   _____

3. How long can you focus on a goal without becoming distracted? (1 day, 1 week, 3 weeks and 2 days, etc.)?

   _____

Once you know how you work and what phrases and actions help you to keep going you know the attitude and tone you need to set. Remember, an attitude refers to the characteristics, feelings, and/or beliefs that a person has and tone refers to how they are delivering their message (even to themselves). By answering the questions above you are determining how you want to see this **S.T.R.E.T.C.H.** presented (as a choice, a positive change, a competitive goal, etc.) and you are also determining the type of reinforcement you need in order to believe, even through the rough patches, that you will accomplish your goal.

You don't have to choose just one of the options, choose as many as you need in order to set yourself up to complete the goal and achieve success.

Stretch Example:
I want to learn how to manage my time better as a mom, wife, daughter, and entrepreneur.
   a. ***Sample Tones (mantras): I get*** *to learn how to manage my time better as a mom, wife, daughter, and entrepreneur.*
   b. ***I'm going to learn how*** to manage my time better as a mom, wife, daughter, and entrepreneur because...I want to have 5 extra hours a week to play with my daughter or because...I want to have a date night with my spouse.
   c. ***I am smart enough*** to learn
   d. ***I am organized enough to learn***

Both ***a*** and ***d*** work the best for me. I ensure I set time aside to regularly work on my goal and I start each of these sessions with my mantras. And because I know that I am externally motivated as much as I am internally motivated, I am going to ensure that I am sharing my progress with someone I trust to both encourage me to keep moving forward and to tell me when I can do better. This means that I keep seeing this goal as something I ***WANT*** to keep moving forward with. Why? Because this goal is important to me, I KNOW that I am organized enough to learn and I will not allow this goal to defeat me.

When you set up your stretch and determine the tone with which you will move forward you are creating the shape of your roadmap for reaching your dreams. The goal is to set a tone of confidence. I AM GOING TO DO THIS. I GET TO DO THIS (this is fun), I AM GOING TO DO THIS, because it will help me get what I want.

Now, write down your tone of choice (include what you want to tell yourself to stay motivated and how often you want to internally reinforce). You can also include who you need to help encourage you and how often you need external reinforcement:

_____

_____

_____

_____

✓ **Check Point Station:** *At the end of each section, we will summarize where we are in our STRETCH process.*

S: Self-Awareness (Identifying what matters to you)

T: Tone (Attitude) (When approaching your stretch goal, what tone and attitude will you choose)?

You now are ready to approach your stretch with empowerment and choice. This is the launching pad you need to propel your next 5 steps to your stretch!

On your mark, get set, GO...

R is for *Reflect* on What Is Needed

Reflect (verb): Introspect. Ponder. Ruminate. Reflect on one's own thoughts and feelings.

When we choose to stretch out of our comfort zone, we can often experience discomfort and a possible, "Well that didn't work" conversation. Unfortunately, many of us decide that the process doesn't work and we quit the stretch and go back to what's comfortable. Even if we know it's not the best choice.

I strongly encourage you to stick with the stretch and stay on the journey. Results are NOT always immediate and they take time, follow-through, and being open to learning.

We just finished setting the tone for your stretch goal. After setting this tone for your future self, you now have to decide what about your life needs to change to make that happen. You can't keep doing the same thing and expect things to get better. That is the very definition of insanity.

Before you can follow through on the vision of where you want to go, you have to assess what is needed to create change. This includes reflection on self-change.

What do you physically and emotionally need to carry out this goal? What are your 'asks'. Are you creating a power promise to just yourself or are you collecting accountability partners? Do you need to learn new skills? Earn certifications? Obtain materials? List the resources, tangible and intangible, that you will need to accomplish this goal.

This phase of exercises will help you prepare to make changes. Prepare yourself to be uncomfortable. Maybe prepare those around you for the change as well. Prepare yourself to give up something in order to get something.

Ask yourself: *(feel free to use the notes pages or brainstorming pages at the end of this workbook)*
1. What is your ultimate intention and purpose?
2. What resources do you need?
3. Determine what you already have and what you need to acquire.
4. What did I learn from my first step of my stretch? From my 2nd step, etc.
5. What can I do next time to improve the result?

Tip:
Gentle reminder: Stretching takes time and practice and is a skill that many high achievers possess.

One part of this phase that many people find uncomfortable is asking for help, or even thinking about accepting help. *Part of reflecting on what's needed is reflecting on what you need from others.* A lot of times we consider it a weakness to ask for help or delegate. And sometimes when someone offers to help us and we want to accept, *we don't even know what is needed.* If you go out and find those who can help you, and understand how their help is needed, you can much better focus your strengths and gifts as part of a masterful group.

Stretch Example:

Self-Awareness: *I want to learn how to manage my time better as a mom, wife, daughter, and entrepreneur.* **Future state**: *When I have learned to manage my time better, this is what it looks like for me: I will be able to be fully present in whichever role I am in. I am energized and ready to deliver in any of these roles; entrepreneur, mom, wife, and daughter. How will I measure my outcome in the end?*

1. *When I have prioritized my tasks for the day in a way that is best for my life that day*
2. *When I consistently feel present and focused on the task at hand*
3. *When I am consistently achieving the priority items on my calendar 5 days out of 7.*
4. *When I am accomplishing goals in one of my roles without feeling frazzled across all 4 roles.*

Tone: *I can choose my attitude and set my tone. Every day I can start my day by looking at my calendar or creating my to-do list. And ensure that I praise and/or reward myself for completing this step towards better managing my time. For those days where I do not achieve this step, I can set the intention to remind myself that tomorrow is a new day and I* **get to** *do better.*

Reflect on what I will need: *To start having a conversation with my husband and daughter so that they know what my intentions are. Setting up scheduled times on my calendar to accomplish my action items, etc. This is super important so that all stakeholders that are impacted by my goal are aware of what it is I am doing and why I am showing up the way I am.*

	Reflect Activity
	Reflect on what's needed

Now, let's figure what is needed for YOU to fulfill your stretch. Write a list of what you need to complete your stretch.

Some things to consider are:

Where will you be working on this goal?
What type of setting you need to execute your steps?

_____

_____

_____

What do you need to be fully *prepared* to act?
Do you need a full 8 hours of sleep to be at your best? Do you need to ensure you've eaten before you sit down to study or exercise or step into the next action to meet your goal?

_____

_____

_____

What do you need from those around you? If someone offers to help you, brainstorm below what you can authentically tell them you may need.

Do you need affirmation, validation, a hug?

_____

_____

_____

Will your stretch affect your income?
Do you need to make sure you are financially secure before taking the next step?

_____

_____

_____

How do you like to measure progress?
Do you need to set milestones to allow you to stay on track and recognize and celebrate your progress?

_____

_____

_____

What type of material needs will you have?
Books, equipment, a specific type of apparel, etc.

_____

_____

_____

Will you need a source from which to learn new skills?
A class, YouTube videos, online courses?

_____

_____

_____

Do you need further training or education?
Is certification needed? What type?

_____

_____

_____

Tip:

Don't forget to list specific resources. Did you remember to include the resources you need? If you need to take a class, below is where you can list potential educational institutions. If you do need those regular hugs, where are you getting them from? It's important to identify the people you may need around you in order to accomplish your goals as well. Is one of your needs a mentor? Then list your possible options. The purpose of this step is to ensure we don't get stuck as we execute our stretch because we didn't take into consideration what was needed to achieve our goal. For example, my current goal is time management. As I started working on this goal I had to determine what I needed. One of those considerations was whether to use a programmatic solution like David Allen's *Getting Things Done* (GTD) or Brendon Burchard's, *The High-Performance Planner*.

Next, let's look at potential road-blocks. We may not be able to see them all in advance but we can identify some of them and plan to avoid or overcome them.

Obstacles

What are some possible obstacles or hurdles you may encounter to achieving your goal?

_____

_____

_____

What is your plan to help you to overcome these obstacles?

_____

_____

_____

Did you know?

"It is said that we make conscious choices only 5% of the time – the other 95% represents just doing things out of habit." (An example of unconscious behavior is breathing).

Check Point Station: *At the end of each section, we will summarize where we are in our STRETCH process.*

S: Self-Awareness (Identifying what matters to you)

T: Tone (Attitude) (When approaching your stretch goal, what tone and attitude will you choose?

R: Reflect on What's Needed (What support do you need from yourself and others to accomplish your goal)?

E is for *Engage* in New Ideas

Now that you know and have identified what you need, it's essential to stay open-minded to different perspectives and tools. Because sometimes in life when we get what we need, it doesn't look the way we expect. So, how do we do that? Exit your comfort zone. This is where you really start S.T.R.E.T.C.H.ing. Explore your options, engage in new ideas. Identify different paths to achieving that goal. Be open to listening to others. Expose yourself to new ways of doing things.

For those goals where it's relevant, collaborating with others could expose you to new options and resources. This is partly because the experiences someone else has had enables them to see the problem differently than you do. This may allow them to help you in ways you might not think for yourself. This is the value of differing perspectives.

Consider a concept like water. One person might picture a running faucet while another may picture the ocean, and another the rain. Or someone may even have water associated with fear if they were harmed by it in some way. No individual's concept is wrong but each is distinct because of their background, past experience of water, and more. When we understand why someone else's ideas differ from our own that's when a real connection can occur.

When you cross-pollinate through brainstorming or asking questions, everyone's information comes together. Everyone knows different pieces of a whole. Starting to listen and engage with what you hear for its own sake is how the entire conversation starts to shift and stretch into something greater.

Gathering different perspectives is not just done by in-person collaboration. Going back to my example in Reflect for identifying resources. Two of the resources I looked at, *Getting Things Done* and *The High-Performance Planner*, look at the same ultimate goal from different perspectives. By evaluating both sources I was able to come up with my own process that is working for me. I would never have thought of some of the methods I am using now if I had not taken a look at what others had to say on the subject.

Now it's your turn.

Stretch Example:

Self-Awareness: *I want to learn how to manage my time better as a mom, wife, daughter, and entrepreneur.* **Future state**: *When I have learned to manage my time better, this is what it looks like for me: I will be able to be fully present in whichever role I am in. I am energized and ready to deliver in any of these roles; entrepreneur, mom, wife, and daughter. How will I measure my outcome in the end?*

1. *When I have prioritized my tasks for the day in a way that is best for my life that day*
2. *When I consistently feel present and focused on the task at hand*
3. *When I am consistently achieving the priority items on my calendar 5 days out of 7.*
4. *When I am accomplishing goals in one of my roles without feeling frazzled across all 4 roles.*

Tone: *I can choose my attitude and set my tone. Every day I can start my day by looking at my calendar or creating my to-do list. And ensure that I praise and/or reward myself for completing this step towards better managing my time. For those days where I do not achieve this step, I can set the intention to remind myself that tomorrow is a new day and I* **get to** *do better.*

Reflect on what I will need: *To start having a conversation with my husband and daughter so that they know what my intentions are. Setting up scheduled times on my calendar to accomplish my action items, etc. This is super important so that all stakeholders that are impacted by my goal are aware of what it is I am doing and why I am showing up the way I am.*

How will I engage in new ideas? *By looking at existing resources on time management, such as the GTD system, the Pomodoro Technique, and relevant time management planners. By surrounding myself with other moms that are successful entrepreneurs and learn from them what worked and what didn't. Also by interviewing other entrepreneurs that come to the table with different experiences from different disciplines.*

	Engage Activity
	Engage in new ideas

Your S.T.R.E.T.C.H. goal:

_____

_____

_____

_____

Based on what your goal is, *design and strategize*:

Depending on whether you chose a personal or professional STRETCH, there are different processes that are used to make it easier to adopt. For example, in the world of business, the SIPOC diagram is a **visual tool for documenting a business process from the beginning to the end.** There are even tools and processes such as Lean Six Sigma used not only in manufacturing or supply chain processes but used in ALL aspects of a business.

1. What kind of research will you need to do to accomplish your goal?

    _____

    _____

    _____

    _____

2. If you can, brainstorm different ideas on a whiteboard or sticky notes. If you have the opportunity to work with others, brainstorm together on different ideas and approaches to accomplish your goal. (There are sheets at the end of this workbook you can use as well.)

3. Identify at least 3 people that you may need to interview in order to advance your *S.T.R.E.T.C.H.* goal forward.

Three People to Interview	
1.	
2.	
3.	

4. What ideas have they shared with you, or what new ideas did you discover while doing your research?

_____

_____

_____

_____

5. Now that you have pulled your ideas and data together, what will be your strategy in order to achieve your stretch goal?

_____

_____

_____

So, what's next? That little push we need to pull it all together and get it done and make it to the finish line! Some options are:

- Have an accountability partner
- Create a self-administrated progress/reward system where you set mini-goals (milestones) and reward yourself for them
- Keep a progress journal that you write in daily, regardless of your progress

It's amazing how the right kind of accountability can provide insight that you may need to make achieving your goal more successful. *How* will you choose to hold yourself accountable? And if you can, *who* will you choose to hold you accountable?

Use this format for your notes to help hold you accountable.

Set your intention (your stretch, your power promise):

_____

What is your next step?

_____

Who is your accountability partner? (Can be yourself or another person)

_____

Your completion date:

_____

Did you know?
According to a study done by *The American Society of Training and Development (ASTD)*, If you have an accountability partner, you're 65% more likely to complete a task and you'll increase your chance of success by up to 95%.

Check Point Station: *At the end of each section, we will summarize where we are in our STRETCH process.*

S: <u>Self-Awareness.</u> Identifying what matters to you.

T: <u>Tone (Attitude)</u> When approaching your stretch goal, what tone and attitude will you choose?

R: <u>Reflect on What's Needed.</u> What support do you need from yourself and others to accomplish your goal?

E: <u>Engage in New Ideas.</u> Exit Your Comfort Zone. Explore your options and identify different paths to achieving your goal(s).

Our biggest challenge is to put in place new positive habits that will help us achieve the things we want in order to be successful. The next section will allow you to take the work you have completed to this point and turn them into action.

T is for Take Action

By now you're starting to understand, stretching out of your comfort zone comes with many responsibilities and hard work. You can just imagine everything you need to do, and need help from others doing, right?

But thinking about stretching and making a change has no value if one doesn't take action. Step into your stretch! Don't let self-doubt keep you from completing your stretch. You worked hard to come this far, stay the course.

Part of why training doesn't move the needle at organizations is participants don't take action to make connections, on both sides of the discomfort, that comes with change. Everyone may be uncomfortable in this growth, but by working through that discomfort the common ground is achieved, and the end result is much better where each person has a chance to be comfortable.

But if you don't have a purpose or set an intention to mutually reach this level of collaboration at an organizational level, can you actually get there?

Part of taking action is identifying who will be impacted by your choices, by your failures, and by your successes. Who has your back? Do you have your own?

"It is impossible to live without failing at something unless you live so cautiously that you might as well have not lived at all." – J.K. Rowling

How is this relevant to your S.T.R.E.T.C.H. goal?

Have you ever created a New Year's Resolution, only to find out that after a few weeks, or months, you lose interest and don't complete your resolution?

I have.

That's because I didn't have a set intention or purpose laid out with a plan of action that also included accountability.

University of Scranton research suggests that just 8% of people achieve their New Year's goals.

So let's look at what separates this 8% percent who DO achieve their goals from the vast majority who don't?

The answer has everything to do with ACTION. And so does this section of your **S.T.R.E.T.C.H.** goal.

Is there a set formula for success? Many people will provide different formulas. I am going to advise you to find what works for you. In this workbook, the formula (tool) that you are using will be able to take you through your **S.T.R.E.T.C.H.** goal and allow you to take consistent action toward realizing your dreams. You learn that by walking through these steps, one by one, and not just a giant singular leap, that your actions will lead to success. Without regular and decisive action, your **S.T.R.E.T.C.H.** goals simply are not going to be achieved. Period.

No matter how ambitious your goals, or how brilliant your plans are for achieving them, if you're not prepared to take regular consistent action to reach them, they're not really goals at all—they're just wishes, fantasies and daydreams. -Jack Canfield

 Stretch Example:

Self-Awareness: *I want to learn how to manage my time better as a mom, wife, daughter, and entrepreneur.* **Future state**: *When I have learned to manage my time better, this is what it looks like for me: I will be able to be fully present in whichever role I am in. I am energized and ready to deliver in any of these roles; entrepreneur, mom, wife, and daughter. How will I measure my outcome in the end?*

1. *When I have prioritized my tasks for the day in a way that is best for my life that day*
2. *When I consistently feel present and focused on the task at hand*
3. *When I am consistently achieving the priority items on my calendar 5 days out of 7.*

4. When I am accomplishing goals in one of my roles without feeling frazzled across all 4 roles.

Tone: I can choose my attitude and set my tone. Every day I can start my day by looking at my calendar or creating my to-do list. And ensure that I praise and/or reward myself for completing this step towards better managing my time. For those days where I do not achieve this step, I can set the intention to remind myself that tomorrow is a new day and I **get to** do better.

Reflect on what I will need: To start having a conversation with my husband and daughter so that they know what my intentions are. Setting up scheduled times on my calendar to accomplish my action items, etc. This is super important so that all stakeholders that are impacted by my goal are aware of what it is I am doing and why I am showing up the way I am.

How will I engage in new ideas? By looking at existing resources on time management, such as the GTD system, the Pomodoro Technique, and relevant time management planners. By surrounding myself with other moms that are successful entrepreneurs and learn from them what worked and what didn't. Also by interviewing other entrepreneurs that come to the table with different experiences from different disciplines.

Take Action: I will choose which tool works best for me and experiment to see what system works best for me. I will then trial what times I can block off on my calendar to designate each of the roles that I play; Being mindful that some of these roles (such as mom, wife, and daughter may intersect). I will give myself permission to add in time for me (yes, I did forget to add that to my initial STRETCH goal, most of us do!)

Tip:

Word of Warning: *Throughout this process, you may come to learn that your original STRETCH goal may not have been your actual intention or goal that you thought you wanted to achieve. How many times do we set a goal just to set it? Like, looking for a new job without knowing WHY you wanted a new job. Are you unhappy with your current job? Do you need more income? Do you not get the personal satisfaction you need to feel valued in your current job? Whatever the reason, you really need to lay out a vision of why you want to apply for a new job. Otherwise, you may job hop for a while. Take a moment to STOP and REFLECT. Because maybe the perfect job may not exist. Maybe the goal could be that the job is not about filling your passion but rather your job may just fill your need for job stability. And then you get to fulfill your passion somewhere else.*

	Take Action Activity
	Action tips

Let's turn your *S.T.R.E.T.C.H.* goal into your success story by filling out these 3 steps of *Action* you can take.

1. **Remove all excuses.** (What excuses have you created that are getting in your way of moving to the next step of action? Please note that just because I am labeling them 'excuses' doesn't mean that I don't realize they are powerful and real in your life, such as money, resources, connections, timing, etc.)

   *Grab a stack of index cards or sticky notes and put one excuse on each card (note).

*Now throw them all away

Tip:

How to successfully complete this tip before going on to the next:
It's easy for each of us to come up with reasons why we can't get something done. We often say, "once I do ABC, then I will do XYZ'" and put off starting something until we feel fully prepared to tackle it. However, to achieve your goals, you must give up all of your excuses because you will always be able to come up with reasons why you should wait before you even start.

Successful people don't listen to those reasons and excuses. And if they do, they invite an accountability partner(s) to hold them accountable. They build their momentum by taking action.

2. Don't wait. Just start.

You don't have to be great to start, but you have to start to be great.
~ Joe Sabah

I love how simple this sounds. And simple it can be. I have a great friend and coach that always tells me, "just start and don't worry about how everything sounds, looks, feels. You can edit as you go along". Trust me, for my personality type, I am always trying to get things to be perfect before I share or launch them. Sad to say, I don't get through all that I need to.

One of the biggest excuses we hear is "I can't find the time." If this is your excuse then you may be trying to take large leaps, when what you need are small steps.

Think of 3 small steps you can take toward your goal that will take 15 minutes or less. List them below:

Three Small Steps Toward Your Goal	
1.	
2.	
3.	

And then do one. If you cannot find 15 minutes to move forward in this goal, then you may want to re-evaluate how important it is to you. You can do this with most excuses we've heard. If money is the issue, then look for free or low cost options. You may even consider bartering for what you need. Bartering is one of my favorite ways to acquire the help I need, whether that help is in the form of tangible items, services or training in a new skill. It is also one of the best ways to expand the group of talented, resourceful people around you.

Now that you are in the mindset to remove the obstacles that you believed were in your way, it's time for you to get started and step into ACTION.

 Did You Know: Facebook and LinkedIn are excellent places for asking for help and advice. If you have an obstacle you don't know how to get around, take it back to the ENGAGE step and ask others for suggestions. You'd be surprised at the wealth of knowledge that is out there if you're only willing to ask.

Your Next Steps:

Take the above "Three Small Steps Toward Your Goal," and copy them below in the left-hand column. Each of those small goals may be broken down into even smaller mini-steps to allow you to reach your ultimate STRETCH goal.

(For example, if your STRETCH goal was to get a new job, then some of the smaller goals may be, to work on your resume, to search for 3 jobs a week, to attend at least 1 networking event/week, etc.)

Three Small Steps Toward Your Goal	Mini-Steps for Small Goals	Due Date

When we provide ourselves with a deadline to achieve our goals, we have a greater success rate in reaching our goals.

Establish a "Due Date" for each of your "Mini-Steps for Small Goals," and record it in the table above.

After you've had a chance to work on your goals, it's valuable to reflect on whether the action you chose successfully brought you closer to your final STRETCH goal.

As you are establishing those due dates, be mindful to schedule "Progress Checks" along the way so that you don't wait for a long period of time to make sure your process is working.

For example, if I set a STRETCH goal to lose 10 pounds in six weeks, I'm not going to wait six weeks to check my weight. I'm going to create weekly "Progress Checks" to ensure the steps I'm taking to reach my goal are successful.

Tip:

Get dates on the calendar. I find it useful to use google calendar to color block out times for different tasks I need to get done. Be mindful of not overbooking yourself.

Tip:

Trial and error. You may discover that when you get to the end of a step or goal that your actions or experiments didn't help you to achieve your desired results, so, you may have to start over. If that is the case, go back to *S is for Self-Awareness*, and redesign your goal. (FYI, this is what usually happens to me and believe it or not, I am empowered by the opportunity to try something different). Don't let this step discourage you or allow self-doubt to creep into your intellectual space. Maybe your goal or tone was right, maybe it *was Reflect on what's needed* that needs to be revisited. However, it shows up, the success is in the 'failure' because you can learn from what you now know! Oh, so powerful!

✓ **Check Point Station:** *At the end of each section, we will summarize where we are in our STRETCH process.*

S: <u>Self-Awareness.</u> Identifying what matters to you.

T: <u>Tone (Attitude)</u> When approaching your stretch goal, what tone and attitude will you choose?

R: <u>Reflect on What's Needed.</u> What support do you need from yourself and others to accomplish your goal?

E: <u>Engage in New Ideas.</u> Exit Your Comfort Zone. Explore your options and identify different paths to achieving your goal(s).

T: <u>Take Action</u>. Step into the stretch and follow through with the extension. Don't let doubt prevent you from completing the stretch you've started. Start with the first step and complete it.

C is for Change Management

According to the Association of Change Management Professional (ACMP)

ACMP defines change management as the practice of applying a structured approach to transition an organization (or a person) from a current state to a future state to achieve expected benefits.

One of the essential parts of stretching is, it's never done. No matter how many times you stretch before a run, you still stretch before the next one too. In much the same way, the next phases are a rinse-repeat of the processes you've already gone through.

As you achieve some goals you'll set new ones and add new tasks to your daily regimen. Other ideas will evolve, some steps will be iterated and improved upon as your future self learns some of the things you don't know now and makes the choice to adapt and improve. Long-term change when done correctly, is often an iterative process. Meaning there is repetition as you improve your processes. Each iteration has its own successes and failures, you keep the positives, dump the negatives, and move on to do it better than before.

Essentially, once the action has been taken you need to record data about outcomes and learn from it. All industries approach this idea the same, but with different terms. What you are looking at is testing your activity and improving based on what comes up.

At this step of your *S.T.R.E.T.C.H.* you have taken action and you need to document your observations and your results. This is when you get to PAUSE. I love pausing! It gives us the opportunity to reflect. Ask yourself, what's working? What's not working? You may even make adjustments to your process based on what feedback others give you. Maybe your first idea for action doesn't take you toward your goal the way you wanted. But whatever you learn will show you a better path. The power of this step is that you get to remind yourself that you are in control of how this is done. What that means is that you can change what this looks like at any given time based on your needs in the present.

Example: *Previously, I used a time management tool that was calendar-based and focused on setting specific blocks of time out. At the time this system worked well for me. However, as my needs changed it became less and less effective and I needed to find another process that worked for me. I was able to take what still worked from that process, eliminate what didn't work, and find a new system that is meeting my needs. I was able to do this by pausing and evaluating and making the needed adjustments to keep my actions in alignment with my goal.*

If you think good design is expensive, you should look at the cost of bad design.
-Ralf Speth

I love this quote for a couple of reasons. Bad design can be expensive, both in materials, time, and emotional energy. How often do we see poorly designed processes negatively impact company morale and culture? With your own personal goals, is it worth it to risk your time and resources by not taking a more iterative approach and pausing to ensure you are still finding value in your current course of action? Or would you prefer to take the time to collect data, invite feedback, and make adjustments to correct course if needed?

Stretch Example:

<u>***Self-Awareness:***</u> *I want to learn how to manage my time better as a mom, wife, daughter, and entrepreneur.* ***Future state****: When I have learned to manage my time better, this is what it looks like for me: I will be able to be fully present in whichever role I am in. I am energized and ready to deliver in any of these roles; entrepreneur, mom, wife, and daughter. How will I measure my outcome in the end?*

1. *When I have prioritized my tasks for the day in a way that is best for my life that day*
2. *When I consistently feel present and focused on the task at hand*

3. *When I am consistently achieving the priority items on my calendar 5 days out of 7.*
4. *When I am accomplishing goals in one of my roles without feeling frazzled across all 4 roles.*

Tone: *I can choose my attitude and set my tone. Every day I can start my day by looking at my calendar or creating my to-do list. And ensure that I praise and/or reward myself for completing this step towards better managing my time. For those days where I do not achieve this step, I can set the intention to remind myself that tomorrow is a new day and I **get to** do better.*

Reflect on what I will need: *To start having a conversation with my husband and daughter so that they know what my intentions are. Setting up scheduled times on my calendar to accomplish my action items, etc. This is super important so that all stakeholders that are impacted by my goal are aware of what it is I am doing and why I am showing up the way I am.*

How will I engage in new ideas? *By looking at existing resources on time management, such as the GTD system, the Pomodoro Technique, and relevant time management planners. By surrounding myself with other moms that are successful entrepreneurs and learn from them what worked and what didn't. Also by interviewing other entrepreneurs that come to the table with different experiences from different disciplines.*

Take Action: *I will choose which tool works best for me and experiment to see what system works best for me. I will then trial what times I can block off on my calendar to designate each of the roles that I play; Being mindful that some of these roles (such as mom, wife, and daughter may intersect). I will give myself permission to add in time for me (yes, I did forget to add that to my initial STRETCH goal, most of us do!)*

Change Management: *I may be able to accomplish my goal as a businesswoman, but was it at the cost of my quality time with my daughter and husband? So, as I collect my data. What's working, what's not working? Did I achieve the desired outcome and as a result, did I disrupt the balance anywhere else in my life? Am I in balance? Am I in harmony? So, during this retrospective, I get to choose if I need to realign my actions to line up with my personal values.*

Change Management Activity

Collect your data

Am I any closer to achieving my goal than when I started?

YES	NO

From zero to 100, (zero being Day 1 and 100 equaling goal accomplished) where would I rank my progress?

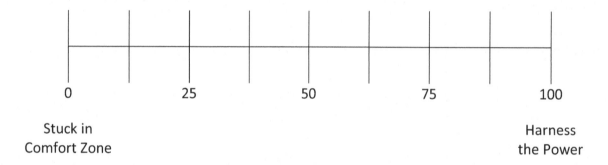

Are your current steps in taking action meeting your needs?

YES	NO

List 3 benefits of your current process and 3 drawbacks of your current process.

Your Current Process	Benefits	Drawbacks

Do I have access to a better way of achieving my goal? If yes, identify it.

YES	Explain:
NO	

What, if anything, needs to change about how I am Taking Action? (Including adjusting the tone I've set if it isn't working)

_____

_____

_____

_____

List at least three steps that you will take after this reflection?

1.

2.

3.

As previously mentioned, and at this point of evaluation, you may discover that what you are doing is not working. That is not uncommon when changes are made. It also does not have to be negative.

One, congratulate yourself on taking the step to make a positive change. You didn't just talk about it you moved toward achieving it!

Two, you learned something. You learned what doesn't work for you. And now you get to use that to find something that does.

Three, there is a reason that stretching increases agility and it isn't because we get things exactly the way we need them with the first stretch. It's because with every stretch it becomes easier to do the next one, and the next, increasing our flexibility and our ability to manage change. Because change is constant.

✓ **Check Point Station:** *At the end of each section, we will summarize where we are in our STRETCH process.*

S: <u>Self-Awareness.</u> Identifying what matters to you.

T: <u>Tone (Attitude)</u> When approaching your stretch goal, what tone and attitude will you choose?

R: <u>Reflect on What's Needed.</u> What support do you need from yourself and others to accomplish your goal?

E: <u>Engage in New Ideas.</u> Exit Your Comfort Zone. Explore your options and identify different paths to achieving your goal(s).

T: <u>Take Action.</u> Step into the stretch and follow through with the extension. Don't let doubt prevent you from completing the stretch you've started. Start with the first step and complete it.

C: <u>Change Management.</u> Collect the data, what's working, what's not working? Evaluate and make adjustments to ensure this path is still leading you towards your goals.

H is for Harness the Power

You have just done something HUGE! You identified a NEED, you determined a course of action AND you followed through. Celebrate your STRETCH out of your comfort zone.

This is just the beginning. Now you get to take what you learned, the confidence you built, and you get to keep stretching. What happens if you didn't complete your S.T.R.E.T.C.H. goal? Maybe it became irrelevant or unattainable due to a life issue. Maybe something else took priority. Or maybe the original goal had to shift a little due to new opportunities in your life. These are not failures, these are learning opportunities. Your goal was set because when you set it made sense. We are not static beings, we change and our lives change. The only way this counts as a failure is if you choose not to learn from the accomplishment you did achieve.

Accomplishment Checklist:
- Did I figure out what tone works to help push me towards achieving a goal?
- Did I do the research to determine whether the goal was feasible and identify the resources I had and needed?
- Did I identify new resources I didn't even know I had?
- Did I step outside of my comfort zone and look into new ways of achieving my goal and other perspectives and thought-leaders in this area?
- Did I take action towards achieving my goal? Were any of the steps I needed to take initiated?
- Did I look at my goal and my progress and evaluate where I was, what I still needed to do, and whether my current process was working for me?

If you can say *Yes* to any of these questions then you accomplished something, whether it was gaining new knowledge or successfully accomplishing your goal.

Whether the win is immediate or well into the next generation, there is a reason for stepping outside of our comfort zone. Growth and Learning. The hardest part of keeping it going is looking for the evidence, right? Often stretching efforts don't become a habit because we want to experience the benefits immediately, we want instant gratification. But, it doesn't work that way. The magic shows up in so many different, small ways.

Sometimes, that's the magic of trying something and hating it. Even then, you learned something that can guide your future decisions. That is why an essential part of this phase is to celebrate, even if you "failed" by common standards.

Focusing on your capability to stretch, reach, and succeed is how you *harness the power.*

I leave you with a sense of empowerment, achievement, and action. Don't let the fear of taking one small step keep you from the possible growth of a huge leap.

Let's celebrate our successes and our failures in both activities below

The power of celebrating success is HUGE!
What are the benefits?

1. Celebrating success strengthens our resiliency
2. Pausing to reflect allows us the space to enjoy the successes we've had so far
3. Feelings of accomplishment provide endorphins which reinforce satisfaction in our work and personal lives
4. It is clinically proven that when we allow ourselves to fully feel, enjoy, and extend our positive experiences, we develop a long-lasting stream of positive thoughts and emotions
5. Success creates more success in the future
6. When we take notice of our past successes we strengthen our confidence in our future successes
7. When we celebrate as a team, we create positive bonds around our combined success
8. When we reflect on how we personally helped achieve an outcome, we see where we are in the bigger picture

Stretch Example:

___

Self-Awareness: *I want to learn how to manage my time better as a mom, wife, daughter, and entrepreneur.* **Future state**: *When I have learned to manage my time better, this is what it looks like for me: I will be able to be fully present in whichever role I am in. I am energized and ready to deliver in any of these roles; entrepreneur, mom, wife, and daughter. How will I measure my outcome in the end?*

1. *When I have prioritized my tasks for the day in a way that is best for my life that day*
2. *When I consistently feel present and focused on the task at hand*
3. *When I am consistently achieving the priority items on my calendar 5 days out of 7.*
4. *When I am accomplishing goals in one of my roles without feeling frazzled across all 4 roles.*

___

Tone: *I can choose my attitude and set my tone. Every day I can start my day by looking at my calendar or creating my to-do list. And ensure that I praise and/or reward myself for completing this step towards better managing my time. For those days where I do not achieve this step, I can set the intention to remind myself that tomorrow is a new day and I **get to** do better.*

___

Reflect on what I will need: *To start having a conversation with my husband and daughter so that they know what my intentions are. Setting up scheduled times on my calendar to accomplish my action items, etc. This is super important so that all stakeholders that are impacted by my goal are aware of what it is I am doing and why I am showing up the way I am.*

___

How will I engage in new ideas? *By looking at existing resources on time management, such as the GTD system, the Pomodoro Technique, and relevant time management planners. By surrounding myself with other moms that are successful entrepreneurs and learn from them what worked and what didn't. Also by interviewing other entrepreneurs that come to the table with different experiences from different disciplines.*

Take Action: *I will choose which tool works best for me and experiment to see what system works best for me. I will then trial what times I can block off on my calendar to designate each of the roles that I play; Being mindful that some of these roles (such as mom, wife, and daughter may intersect). I will give myself permission to add in time for me (yes, I did forget to add that to my initial STRETCH goal, most of us do!)*

Change Management: *I may be able to accomplish my goal as a businesswoman, but was it at the cost of my quality time with my daughter and husband? So, as I collect my data. What's working, what's not working? Did I achieve the desired outcome and as a result did I disrupt the balance anywhere else in my life? Am I in balance? Am I in harmony? So, during this retrospective, I get to choose if I need to realign my actions to line up with my personal values.*

Harness the Power: *You've just done something huge! You identified a need, determined your course of action and you followed through. Celebrate your stretch out of your comfort zone. This is just the beginning. Now you get to take what you've learned, the confidence you've built, and keep the stretch going. What are you going to tackle next?*

Harness the Power Activity

Celebrate your experience

Write down your success. If you're stumped refer to the previous accomplishment checklist.

_____

_____

_____

Take a minute to reflect on how it makes you feel to see your successes written out? Describe that feeling:

_____

_____

_____

Is there anything you see on your list of accomplishments that you didn't realize before?

_____

_____

_____

How do you like to celebrate your accomplishments?

_____

_____

_____

Tip:

Take time out to celebrate even the small wins, the way you celebrate the big wins. Take your list of accomplishments and share it with someone else, whether privately or on Facebook, share it with someone and let them celebrate with you. Share what you wrote, both the struggle and the way you beat it, with others. Let your struggle empower others to keep moving forward to be better than they are today.

Write down one thing you struggled with and overcame during this process:

_____

_____

_____

✓ **Check Point Station:** *At the end of each section, we will summarize where we are in our STRETCH process.*

S: <u>Self-Awareness.</u> Identifying what matters to you.

T: <u>Tone (Attitude)</u> When approaching your stretch goal, what tone and attitude will you choose?

R: <u>Reflect on What's Needed.</u> What support do you need from yourself and others to accomplish your goal?

E: <u>Engage in New Ideas.</u> Exit Your Comfort Zone. Explore your options and identify different paths to achieving your goal(s).

T: <u>Take Action</u>. Step into the stretch and follow through with the extension. Don't let doubt prevent you from completing the stretch you've started. Start with the first step and complete it.

C: <u>Change Management.</u> Collect the data, what's working, what's not working? Evaluate and make adjustments to ensure this path is still leading you towards your goals.

H: <u>Harness the Power.</u> You've just done something huge! You identified a need, determined your course of action and you followed through.
Celebrate your stretch out of your comfort zone. This is just the beginning. Now you get to take what you've learned, the failures you may have experienced, the confidence you've built, and keep the stretch going. What are you going to tackle next?

tru you, llc
Page 60

Note from Sonal:

I am so proud of you! You have successfully taken a journey to step out of your comfort zone. Whether it was for something personal or professional, big or small, you did it. Whether you had self-doubt creep up and challenge you along the way, or outside influences that may have kept you from wanting to move forward, you didn't let it stop you. You pushed through!

It has been throughout my personal and professional journey that I have learned that when I feel overwhelmed by a goal that I set or one that has been set for me, then I need to revisit it and break it down. It's a beautiful thing when we can look at what matters to us from a different lens. From a different perspective. Sometimes even from a neutral perspective.

I have people often ask me; Why does it matter if I stretch out of my comfort zone? Why is it recommended that I use a process or tool? How does this *STRETCH TOOL* even work? How long does it take? How can I measure my success?

I love these questions because, honestly, there are so many different answers. Whether your goal is to try a different type of food, learn how to ride a bike as an adult (that's me), go camping and not glamping (that's me too), apply for a job that you didn't think you were ready for, share your voice at the next meeting at work so people can hear your ideas, invite a colleague for coffee to discuss what they do and how it connects to what you do, go to a networking event to meet more people or to ask someone out that you have been wanting to go out with, forever. The list of *STRETCH* goals can be endless. But what the common denominator is the commitment to want to set a goal and to want to achieve it. The commitment to step into these STEPS as a tool to help you to break down that goal into smaller goals and then to set up progress checks along the way to make sure that you are happy with your process. As for timing? It really depends on the goal that you choose. If you are applying this tool to try a new type of food, well, the process may be within a couple of hours before you *harness the power*. If you set a goal to lose 10 pounds in 6 weeks, well your timing to *harness the power*, will be in 6 weeks. And if you are setting the goal to change career paths, then the time it will take to achieve this will depend on what time frame you would like to change jobs. There is not a specific time allocated to a goal other than the one you assign to it. The thing is, once you commit to step into that STRETCH goal, then have the courage to step into your self-awareness to discover your *WHY.*

I hope your journey of STRETCHING energize you, exhausts you, surprises you, and helps you to discover what really matters to you. And that you can CELEBRATE that you have you have just done something huge! You identified a need, determined your course of action, followed through and you celebrated your stretch out of your comfort zone. What an amazing accomplishment!

I want to start by saying Thank You! Thank you for showing up and committing to stepping into something that you may have felt uncomfortable to do.

This is just the beginning. Now you get to take what you've learned, the confidence you've built, and keep the stretch going. What are you going to tackle next?

Stay Healthy and Keep Stretching,

tru you, llc
Page 62

Some STRETCH Resources

I wanted to be able to share some of the resource links for what I have discovered along my STRETCH journey.

Disclaimer: There are MANY tools out there that work. There are also many tools out there that do not have the research behind them to support them. Please know that the tools that I have listed below are just some that I recommend. I do not represent nor belong to any of these organizations. I have just found some of these online and they worked for me.

Self-Awareness:
1. http://personalitypokergame.com/
2. https://greatergood.berkeley.edu/quizzes/take_quiz/gratitude
3. https://www.6seconds.org/2018/02/27/emotional-intelligence-tips-awareness/

Free Emotional Intelligence Quiz:
1. https://www.ihhp.com/free-eq-quiz/
2. https://www.mindtools.com/pages/article/ei-quiz.htm

Tools to help you Plan:
1. Pomodoro Technique: https://www.focusboosterapp.com/pomodoro-technique-planning
2. Getting things Done tool: https://gettingthingsdone.com/
3. The High-Performance Planner by Brendon Burchard: https://hpxwellness.mykajabi.com/high-performance-planner?gclid=Cj0KCQjwpNr4BRDYARIsAADIx9zBW6t84RY6Y6DjUDAERxnIdnK_r83yO1z8I-LARoBOrtxLP5PFJXYaAoukEALw_wcB

Interview with Sonal

Sonal, tell me about your journey to NOW.

My family immigrated to the states in 1971. I was raised in a community in Brooklyn, where everyone lived together, worked together, experienced together. Where people didn't see color. Being an immigrant family coming from India, taking care of four kids with only $7 gave my family an appreciation for differences, similarities, and the diversity of people who are here right now.

Even when times were tough, people celebrated and mourned together. That's what I learned by being in the community that I was raised in. That's what my parents showed me by moving to America, and that's what I was used to. And that is what I brought to my life in the Midwest when my family relocated to Oxford, Ohio at the age of 12 in 1982.

So, fast forward a decade, and I brought this rich experience into my classroom as a high school science teacher, into my consulting where I trained teachers to become well-rounded teachers, into my leadership as a Director of Education. I also brought it into my relationships with the professors I advised while at Wiley publishing, and now as I train companies and coach leaders. As I train leaders on Emotional Intelligence, Communication, Leadership, Diversity and Inclusion and how to support and guide people to stretch out of their comfort zone. As I remind everyone that they are leaders too, regardless of their title.

I am inclusive. That's what my friends and community tell me! I have a tribe of men and women, a huge community, that look different, think a bit different, are of different ages, races and stages in life, and, yet, they are all part of the same planning committee. Each of them may have different political and home cultures, but they all share the same values in life. It is my innate need, my instincts to make sure that all the people in my life know each other and are brought together so they can share their lives, their stories! I ensure that they celebrate holidays, birthdays and even the difficult times together with my entire personal family; my parents, siblings, husband, and daughter. I firmly believe WE are all in this together!

And I am the hub.

"Diversity is going to a party and inclusion is being a member of the party planning committee" -Dr. Daniel Juday

Take a look, who is on your planning committee?

Sonal, how can I build a team of support around me to encourage me to stretch?

My friends like to remind me that I am a people collector and connector. Whether you are someone who is an introvert or an extrovert, you can still build a team of support. I think the stereotype is that extroverts must have a large circle of support and introverts don't. That's not always how it is. We know to be true, through experience, that there are many extroverts that are not necessarily always great with people and introverts that are. This is where Emotional Intelligence comes in handy. As long as you are self-aware as to who you are and what matters to you, you will then be able to manage how you show up in order to connect with others. This is what will allow you to build strong relationships and a team of support.

I am definitely an extrovert that is energized by being around people. So, I make it my intention to attend various types of networking events, both in and out of my industry so that I can collect and connect with people of all backgrounds and perspectives. It really has stretched me out of my comfort zone, yet as been invigorating and life learning to experience so many different people.

Sonal, why are you so focused on STRETCHING?

I always wanted to be a motivational speaker and trainer. I've been dreaming about this as long as I can remember. That's why I joined the ASTD and Coaching Federation in 2003 when I wasn't even forecasting that I would start my own business doing just that.

Four years ago, I was hanging out with a group of friends that had the courage to listen to me complain about not loving my job and how I wanted to be a TED talk speaker. One of them (now my thinking partner) looked at me and said, Then do it!" I argued with her that it wasn't possible, especially because I have a job and a new baby. But, she challenged me to write a practice TED talk that I can present it to a small focus group in my community. So I did. I prepared and practiced and presented a very well thought out, very informative talk about The power of Communication. The group had very positive feedback but they said it didn't have the Sonal-spark that they are used to. So, I told them that I had an idea for a talk that I had not prepared, that I had a dream about the week before. They told me to try it out on them. They encouraged me to step out of my comfort zone and just speak my soul. And so I did. That talk was 'Have you stretched today." A concept that I had a dream about because I was afraid to step out of my comfort zone and into a space where my passions lived. When that talk was over, the room was silent because the audience was just blown away about how vulnerable, authentic, informative, relatable, and passionate I was. Since then I have been amazed at the power of the message of 'Have you stretched today'

Sonal, what qualifies you to be a motivational speaker and trainer?

Oh, this question... yuck! This question makes me uncomfortable because I don't like to feel like I am bragging. But, also, I don't necessarily feel that people always need qualifiers in order to make an impact. I was raised in a traditional Indian home where discipline and academics dominates in our culture. I truly believe that in addition to my degrees, trainings and certifications that my biggest qualifier is my passion and life experiences of stretching out of my comfort zone and having to start from scratch many times.

If you want to learn more about my background and credentials, feel free to look me up on LinkedIn and let me know if you have any questions!

https://www.linkedin.com/in/sonalshethzawahri/

or check out my website:

https://www.haveyoustretchedtoday.com

Sonal, how can I follow you? What other products do you have? How can someone schedule you to speak?

I am on LinkedIn, Instagram, Facebook and my website. You can always search for me under my full name, (which is my brand), Sonal Sheth Zawahri.

My website offers other publications and products that I have created and can keep you up to speed on what I am doing next. You can even listen to my interviews on

different podcasts as well as many of my keynote and training talks. Also connect with me to schedule.

On the "Work with Sonal" page of my website, you will learn more about and have access to information regarding the Coaching, Training and Workshop Series services I have available.

Currently available on the shop page of my Have you stretched today website; you can find my following products:

1. *Mentoring Moments: 14 Remarkable Women Share Breakthroughs to Success published book*
2. *Val-U Card Deck of Cards: 30 card deck that will provide you with 30 unique expressions of appreciation to ALL your colleagues in your organization*
3. *Have you stretched today? Wrist Bands*

In partnership with my Thinking Partner, Aisha Cargile, I have an additional website where you can access Compliment card decks that you can share with all humans in your life. Check out our website at
https://www.colorfulbosses.com/

Sonal's Shop

When was the last time you really wanted to tell someone on your team or in your organization how you much you valued their contribution, but you either didn't know how to say it or you simply didn't get a chance to do so? Val-U cards provide a unique opportunity to deliver a tangible expression of your appreciation. They are designed to acknowledge the talent and hard work of the people in your organization.

This 30 card deck will provide you with 30 unique expressions of appreciation, that will allow you to communicate to each person how you experience and Val-U them. These cards were made to be shared. Hand them to, or leave them for, those people in your life you truly value.

Need more ideas? Let me know. I'm here to help.

COMPLIMENT CARDS

Show Appreciation.
Build Connections.
Spread Joy.

Origin Story

Colorful bosses started as a way to provide resources to anyone who wanted be a positive force in the world. Separately the creators of colorful bosses work with individuals, corporations and non-profit organizations on doing more, being better and making an impact within their communities. Together they create ways for the quietest introvert to the most outgoing extrovert to have a positive immediate impact on those around them.

For more wonderful products, visit
https://www.sonalshethzawahri.com/shop

Why Sonal?

Improve communication skills | Build stronger leaders and leadership teams
Stretch out of your comfort zone and into new opportunities | Become more strategic in thoughts and actions
Empower others to be better and do more | Discover your purpose

Popular Sessions:

✳ Have You Stretched Today ✳ Emotional Intelligence ✳ Strategic Thinking ✳ Effective Communication
✳ How E.I. Fosters Diverse Workplaces ✳ Leading Without Authority ✳ Active Listening
✳ Step Into Your Power ✳ Empowerment Techniques ✳ Finding Your Purpose

Workshop Series:

Multi-session workshop series that combine tools and topics to achieve targeted outcomes.
Each of the series takes on one of the following organizational issues and stages:

✳ Communication ✳ Collaboration ✳ Cultivation ✳ Motivation ✳ Innovation

---

"I have had the opportunity to attend Sonal's EI vs. IQ presentation. Sonal's subject knowledge and very interactive activities made her concepts come to life. Sonal's presentation draws the audience in and leaves them armed with practical and actionable takeaways."
Faith McKinney, TV Producer, Author

"I had the pleasure of attending one of Sonal's signature PURPOSE creation meetings. Our newly formed department had a subset of five different areas but never really worked together as a cohesive unit- until we met Sonal! By the end of the day we walked away with a collective purpose & knowing how we each contribute to the big picture. Thank you Sonal for helping us see our collective PURPOSE!"
Angel Henry, IT Manager, (KAR Auction)

Sonal blends the wisdom of the industry's most well-known resources with a fascinating bevy of personal and professional experiences to create an energizing and customized event.
-Jason Ward, President, RocketBuild

Celebrate your people, show them how you Val-U Them!

Purchase on website at:
haveyoustretchedtoday.com

Brainstorm Here

A space to generate ideas to resolve problems and overcome roadblocks.

Brain Dump

A place to jot down ideas.

Doodle Page
A place to let your creative juices flow.

tru you, llc
Page 77

Are you ready to have a transformational experience and stretch outside of your comfort zone?

S Step into awareness

T Tone (Attitude)

R Reflect on what's needed

E Engage in new ideas

T Take action

C Change management

H Harness the power

© TRU YOU LLC

DenolaBurton@EnhancedDNA1.com

www.EnhancedDNAPublishing.com